STAY POSITIVE

HOW TO UNLOCK YOUR INNER OPTIMIST

SOPHIE GOLDING

STAY POSITIVE

An Hachette UK Company
www.hachette.co.uk

Vie Books, an imprint of Summersdale Publishers Ltd
Part of Octopus Publishing Group Limited
Carmelite House
50 Victoria Embankment
LONDON
EC4Y 0DZ
UK

www.summersdale.com

Printed and bound in China

ISBN: 978-1-78685-770-5

Substantial discounts on bulk quantities of Summersdale books are available to corporations, professional associations and other organizations. For details contact general enquiries: telephone: +44 (0) 1243 771107 or email: enquiries@summersdale.com.

CONTENTS

POSITIVITY BASICS

THINK POSITIVE TO BE POSITIVE

With the rapid pace of modern life and all the obstacles it throws our way, it can be easy to focus on the negatives. But it needn't be this way! This book is here to help you banish the dark clouds and focus on the good. A positive outlook is all down to the way we think, and there are a whole host of ways to bring this attitude of optimism into your life. From simple ways to boost your mood to tips and ideas to bring the sunshine into your life, this book will endow you with the powers of positivity and help you to become your brightest, happiest self.

It's never too late – never too late to start over, never too late to be happy.

Jane Fonda

FIVE GOOD EVENTS

Our brains process negative and positive events in different ways. This phenomenon has been studied numerous times and it has been found that negative experiences are processed more thoroughly than positive ones, which means that we feel the impact of a setback much more strongly than we feel the effect of positive progress. In other words, we're more likely to remember the bad things than the good.

However, it's not all bad news, because it's also thought that five good events can outweigh the effects of one bad event. When you start to look, you can see brilliant things everywhere, so:

1. Don't beat yourself up for seeing problems, or for taking criticism or bad experiences to heart – everyone does this.

2. Most importantly, remind yourself to look for and enjoy all the many wonderful things that happen all the time, every day.

A positive thought can carry you for hundreds of miles.

There is nothing either good or bad, but thinking makes it so.

William Shakespeare

GET TO KNOW YOUR HAPPY CHEMICALS

There are four main neurochemicals that are released in our brains when we feel happy, and we can deliberately trigger these chemicals to make us feel good.

Dopamine motivates us to act. It is what drives us to fulfil our desires, and it gives us a surge of pleasure when we achieve them. Always having a goal or goals you are working towards will keep your dopamine levels topped up.

Serotonin flows when we feel significant – either loved or important. Many antidepressants focus on increasing serotonin production. Reflecting on past achievements and happiness, and what you have to be grateful for, can encourage the brain to release more serotonin.

Oxytocin creates a feeling of trust and intimacy and is essential for creating strong emotional bonds. It is released by mothers during childbirth and breastfeeding, and by men and women during orgasm. Oxytocin also flows when we give or receive a hug or a gift.

Endorphins reduce our perception of stress and pain, and they are the chemicals that give us a "second wind" and the "runner's high". Perhaps the easiest way to produce endorphins is through laughter or exercise.

The journey of a thousand miles begins with a single step.

Lao Tzu

COME BACK TO NOW

A study published in the *Public Library of Science* peer-reviewed journal *(PLoS ONE)* has shown that the way we think determines the impact that negative events have on us. By taking control of your thoughts, you can put yourself in a more positive mindset. So, if you're going down a negative train of thought, bring yourself back to the present moment. Are you worrying about something you said or did? Or are you scared about something that might happen?

STOP!

And come back to now.

There are two simple techniques that can help you do this:

Take in the world around you. Spend a couple of minutes taking everything in. What can you hear within five paces of you, and what can you hear in the distance? What are those smells? Can you feel the warmth of the sun or the dampness of rain? Watch passing people as they come and go.

Just breathe. Focus on your breaths, and take them a little deeper than normal. Feel the air going through your nose and down to your belly, and experience releasing it again.

Look at the sparrows; they do
not know what they will do in the
next moment. Let us literally live
from moment to moment.

Mahatma Gandhi

ATTITUDE OF GRATITUDE

Counting your blessings helps you feel more positive as it increases your serotonin levels. Keeping a gratitude journal is a remarkably effective way to do this. It's easy: at the end of every day, simply write down some of the good things that have happened. It could be one thing or it could be five. It won't be long before you feel an increased sense of gratitude and positivity, and have a journal full of happy memories.

SEPARATING FICTION FROM FACT

Negative thoughts are often not based on reality. The next time you find yourself worried or angry about something, try to separate facts from fiction. These tips from Travis Bradberry, one of the co-creators of *The Emotional Intelligence Appraisal*, show you how:

- Write down what you are saying to yourself, and then look at it and see if it is true.

- Look out for words such as always, worst, never. For instance, are you really always late? Can an upcoming presentation or social event really be the worst thing you'll ever experience? It is very unlikely that you are late to every single thing, or that your event will be as terrible as you think.

- Now you've written these things down you can think rationally about them. If you are often late, why is this and how can you change it in future? If you're worried about an event, always remember that even if it does go badly, it will end and you will survive – and as it hasn't happened yet, you can't say how it will go.

- If your thoughts still seem like facts, ask a trusted friend to look at them and see if they agree. The truth will not be as negative as you think.

- Identifying your thoughts as just thoughts, not facts, will help break the vicious circle of negativity and allow positive thinking to flourish.

REPLACE THE NEGATIVE
WITH A POSITIVE

Once you've identified your patterns
of negative thinking, it can help to
pick a positive thought to focus on.
Something that happened earlier
today, last week or that's coming
up in the future are all good. Keep
coming back to this thought every
time your brain wanders into
negative territory, and you will train
your brain to have a positive focus.

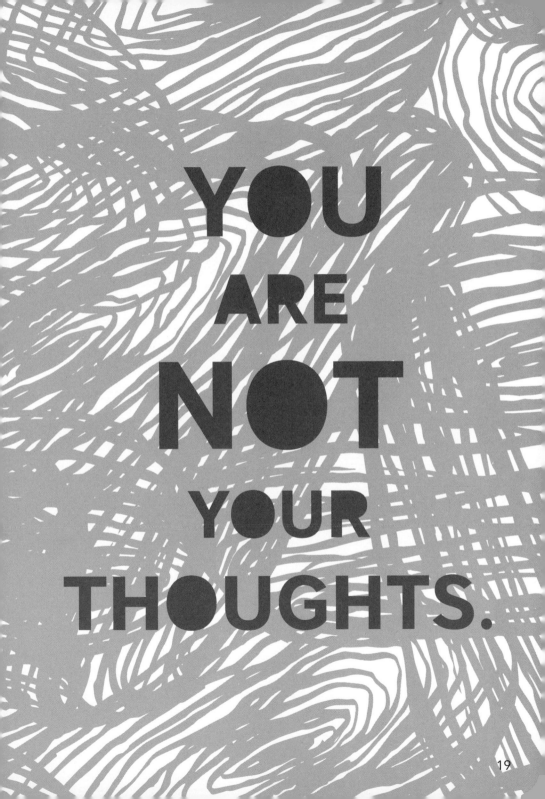

YOU ARE NOT YOUR THOUGHTS.

ONCE A WEEK

Writing down the good things in your life can be rewarding, but if doing this every day seems a challenge, taking stock even just once a week can help boost positivity too. Why not make time to share what you are grateful for with friends or family around the dinner table, or take time on a Sunday to think back over all the good things that happened over the last seven days?

Don't take the basics for granted

Sometimes it's good to remind ourselves how lucky we are that our basic needs are being met. If you have these things in your life, then life is good:

Regular meals.

A roof over your head.

Clean water from a tap.

Electricity and heating.

Friends and family.

Get comfortable with being uncomfortable

There will always be times when we struggle in life, particularly when we go through periods of change, like moving home, divorce or bereavement. In order for anything to improve for the better, there will usually be some discomfort and uncertainty, and if you can accept that change is part of life, the big changes will be easier to deal with. You can build up your tolerance for change by stepping outside of your comfort zone more frequently. Start off simply by trying new things, for instance, taking a different route to work, trying a new café or sampling a food you haven't tasted before. If you're feeling more adventurous, try new experiences that have daunted you in the past – volunteer for a charity you're passionate about, try out for a team sport or sign up for art classes. Every time you step outside of your comfort zone by doing something fun you'll feel a boost of feel-good chemicals, and being able to handle these smaller breaks from routine will help prepare you for the bigger changes in life.

A POSITIVE START

Start your day as you mean to go on by putting a positive reminder by your bed (a photograph of a loved one or a positive affirmation or mantra, perhaps), or by putting on your favourite music and dancing your way into the day.

Be thankful for
what you have;
you'll end up
having more.

Oprah Winfrey

THE BEST THINGS IN LIFE ARE FREE: HUGS, SMILES, FRIENDS AND FAMILY, LOVE, LAUGHTER AND GOOD MEMORIES.

FIND THE SILVER LINING

Look for the positives in everything;
even the most negative situation
can have a silver lining. When
things go wrong, ask yourself:

*What have I learnt from this
situation? Have I gained anything?*

Has anyone shown you unexpected
kindness? Are any of your relationships
stronger? Do you know what
you'd do differently next time?

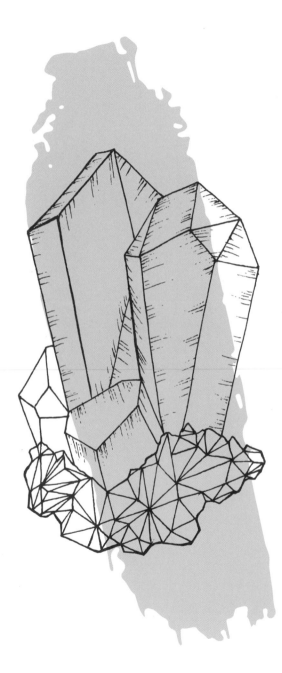

YOUR BRILLIANT LIFE TO COME

Take some time to think about the great things you want for your future. Visualize them or, even better, write them down. Imagine how it will feel to achieve these goals, and remember this positive feeling. Come back to it when you're feeling down for an instant boost.

TURN YOUR FACE TO THE SUN AND THE SHADOWS FALL BEHIND YOU.

Maori proverb

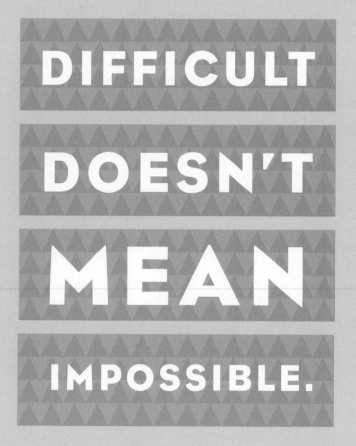

DIFFICULT DOESN'T MEAN IMPOSSIBLE.

SLOW DOWN

Modern life can be frantic, but if you go
about things too fast, stress builds up
and it can be hard to see things clearly.
Take a few moments each day to slow
down, take some deep breaths and
get your body and mind back in sync.
When you're feeling calm and centred
it is much easier to find the positive.

A problem shared is a problem halved

Research published in *Social Psychological and Personality Science* shows that talking to someone in the same situation as you, and who is in a similar emotional state, can be particularly beneficial. If you're feeling stressed, worried or sad, find a support group in your local area, or reach out to a friend or relative who will understand what you're feeling and help share the burden.

Don't judge yourself by
your past.
You don't live there
any more.

Keep moving forward

Setbacks happen to everyone. But when misfortune occurs, don't waste time and energy resisting what is happening and asking, "Why me?" Instead, adopt a positive mindset: accept the reality you are faced with, even if it's uncomfortable, and focus your energy on what you can do to move forward.

There are always flowers for
those who want to see them.

Henri Matisse

EVERY DAY IS NEW.

Take a deep breath and start again.

SIMPLE PLEASURES

GET OUTSIDE

Being in nature is fantastic for boosting positivity. Not only does it reduce stress and calm the mind, it restores energy, strengthens our immune system, sharpens our focus and benefits our short-term memory, and helps maintain our vision – it even keeps us alive for longer. And we're learning more about the amazing health benefits of the great outdoors every day. Recent research published in *BioScience* has shown that a single "exposure to nature" – for instance, a morning walk through the park or pottering around the garden – boosts your positivity for the next seven hours. So what are you waiting for – get outside!

Find ecstasy in life; the mere sense of living is joy enough.

Emily Dickinson

FOREST BATHING

Shinrin-yoku, or "bathing in the forest", is a Japanese practice that is just catching on in the West, and is the simple act of being around trees. Walk slowly in any forest, park or woodland area and engage with all your senses – sight, hearing, taste, touch and smell. Touch the bark of the trees, feel the waxy leaves, sit beneath the boughs and absorb the quiet and calming atmosphere of the forest. Being at one with nature, surrounded by a naturally beautiful ambience, promotes positivity and happiness.

FIND YOUR OWN FEAST

Foraging is a great outdoor activity for the weekend; it's free and you can eat what you find – what could be more satisfying? All these can be found, and more:

- Raspberries, blackberries, bilberries and wild strawberries can all be eaten raw, cooked in crumbles or made into jam.

- Wild garlic, chickweed and clover heads can be used in salad, and nettles can be gathered for soup

- Crab apples, rowan berries and rosehips make great jams and jellies.

- Chestnuts can be roasted and eaten as they are, or added to pies, soups and salads.

Make sure you have permission from the landowner before you forage and, before consuming anything you find, ensure that you have correctly identified it. Gather berries from above "dog toilet" height, and make sure to leave much more than you take for other animals and people. Visit the Woodland Trust website if you would like more information.

THE NATURAL
LUNCH HOUR

This lunchtime, get outside for a wander. Look up at the sky. Can you see any birds or other wildlife? Appreciate the detail of the trees and the strength and stillness of the roots. Notice the flowers. Which have just come out? Which are attracting the most bees? Really looking at the natural world around us creates a sense of calm, connectivity and happiness.

IF IT'S RAINING,

SPLASH

IN THE

PUDDLES.

I would always rather be happy than dignified.

Charlotte Brontë

HAPPY TWEETERS

If you can't always go out into green spaces,
bring nature to you by putting a birdfeeder
or bird food near a window where you often
sit. Enjoy watching the birds come and go,
bicker and feed, knowing that you're also
helping them survive the cold months.

Happiness,
not in another
place, but this
place... not for
another hour, but
for this hour.

Walt Whitman

A MANIFESTO FOR
A HAPPY LIFE:

Eat less, move more.

Buy less, make more.

Stress less, laugh more.

Feel blessed, love more.

Find a quiet spot and breathe.

LEARN TO PLAY AGAIN

It's not just kids who should play – it's important for adults as well! Not only is it fun, but it stimulates your imagination and problem-solving abilities and boosts your emotional well-being. To feel the greatest benefits, play should involve at least one other person, and be away from electronic gadgets. Throw a Frisbee in the park. Play rounders or French cricket. Take colleagues out to play pool or sing karaoke. Host a regular charades or board-game night with family or friends. Playing triggers the release of endorphins, relieving stress. It improves brain function and stimulates learning and creativity. It can deepen friendships, fostering empathy and trust, and it keeps you feeling young and energetic.

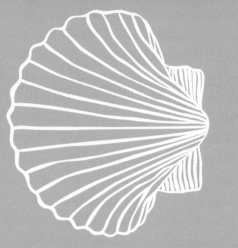

WILD ART

Combine nature with imagination and create art in the wild. Make patterns with leaves of different shapes and colours, arrange stones and pebbles in different patterns or find the most pleasing combination of shells and driftwood. Letting your mind wander as you create, and giving yourself time to relax and unwind, will leave you feeling refreshed and restored. When you've finished, leave your artwork in place for others to enjoy, and then for the wind and rain to slowly take it back into the wild.

GO OFFLINE

The ability to receive emails and access social media on the go is a double-edged sword – at times extremely useful, but studies have shown that smartphone addiction can create imbalances in gamma-aminobutyric acid, one of the body's key neurotransmitters, which in turn cause tiredness, a low mood and severe anxiety. The good news is that most of us can easily make the decision to turn our devices off, and just taking a short break can give you fresh perspective, helping you to be more relaxed and engaged with your surroundings. Switching off and spending quality time with friends and family, without distractions, will make you all feel better connected, and so happier and more fulfilled.

SING A SONG

Singing can reduce stress, improve your posture, boost your immune system and even increase life expectancy – and it definitely makes you feel good, so sing! Whether it's in the shower, in the car or at a karaoke night. You could even join a choir – rock or choral – and sing with others for an extra feel-good boost.

Memories of love

It has recently been discovered that nostalgia is beneficial to our happiness and self-esteem. Fred Bryant, professor of psychology at Loyola University, has described it as a form of mental time travel, as we're seemingly able to go into our past and bring those feelings back into our present. When we reminisce, we are reminded that we love and are loved. We rediscover our strengths, how we coped with difficult situations, and reminiscing gives our lives purpose and meaning. A creative way to recollect the past is to get all those smartphone photos printed – then arrange them in an album or in a frame, and you can return to them whenever you need a boost.

A RELAXING BATH

Sometimes you simply need a little "me time". Run a bath and add some bubbles or salts, and maybe an aromatherapy oil of your choice. Put on some calming music or just enjoy the silence – and relax.

WHOEVER IS HAPPY WILL MAKE OTHERS HAPPY TOO.

Anne Frank

MAGIC MIX-TAPE

Whether you call it a mix-tape or a playlist, put together your favourite feel-good music, and then you always have it on hand for an instant boost of happiness.

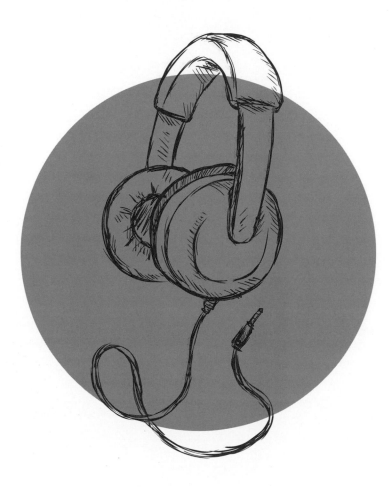

PODCAST POSITIVITY

Transform the chore of housework or a long commute into "positive time" just for you by listening to podcasts. Podcasts are a mine of information and there is something out there for everyone – from meditation to life coaching, humour to inspiration, there are hundreds of high-quality, life-enhancing podcasts available, and all for free.

The body heals
with play, the
mind heals with
laughter and
the spirit heals
with joy.

Proverb

ALL YOU HAVE TO DO

is believe that you can.

Optimism is the faith that
leads to achievement.

Helen Keller

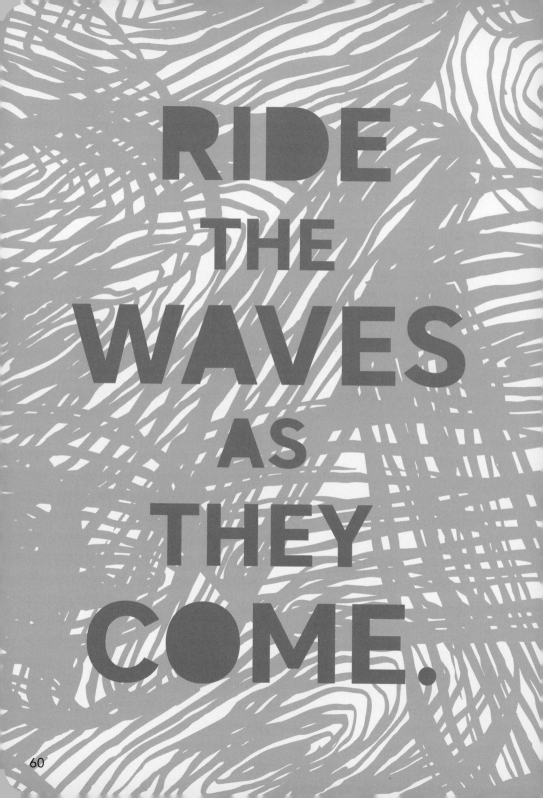

RIDE THE WAVES AS THEY COME.

Just ten breaths

If you feel overwhelmed, frustrated or angry, find a place where you can sit quietly for a few minutes on your own. Close your eyes, then take ten deep breaths. Focus on the air as it enters your body and imagine it taking your stress away with it as it leaves. Gradually, your heart rate will slow, your body will relax and your mind will become calm.

GLOW WITH THE FLOW

Have you ever experienced the feeling of being completely focused on what you're doing, and so absorbed in it that you don't notice time passing? Mihaly Csikszentmihalyi calls this feeling "a state of flow". In his book on the subject, he describes how the mind can only process 126 bits of information per second, and how when having a conversation you use only about 40 of those bits. This leaves over 80 bits to pay attention to other things, which might include negative thoughts. But if you are doing something that is totally absorbing, it takes up all of your attention. This is what is meant by "a state of flow".

It's that feeling of complete immersion when your challenges closely match your abilities – that loss of a sense of time when your actions merge with your awareness. Flow is best achieved when performing anything that requires active participation, and when there are clear goals and instant feedback. It is most attainable when doing a pursuit you love.

What do you love doing that enables you to reach a state of flow?

KEEP YOUR
GOALS FLOWING

Create new goals before you finish
your current one to ensure that
you have a continual stream of
motivating dopamine keeping you
going. Make time to celebrate each
achievement when it happens, and
be a good friend by helping others
celebrate their achievements too.

Food boost

When you look after your body, you look after your mind too. Protein-rich foods, such as fish, chicken and almonds, and complex carbohydrates, like root vegetables, beans and wholegrains, help to increase energy and improve your mood and concentration. For the best state of mind, aim to eat a variety of vegetables, fruit, protein and whole grains.

I may have
been cut
down today,
but I will
flower again
tomorrow.

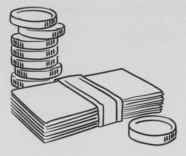

GIVE TO FEEL GOOD

After basic needs such as housing and food are met, studies have shown that the way we spend the rest of our money affects our happiness levels more than how much we earn. In particular, spending money on others is a great way to feel positive. A recent study in *PLoS ONE* suggests that "prosocial bonuses" – where the employer gives bonuses to the whole team or to charities – are much more rewarding to employees than individual cash bonuses. The reason for this is still being studied, but it's thought that the act of giving strengthens and builds new relationships, reduces feelings of competition and suspicion, and acts as a buffer to stress. So, if you've had a little financial bonus, have a little leftover money at the end of the month or you are simply planning your weekly budget, think about who could benefit from what you can spare? By giving money away, even if it's only a few pounds, you'll also benefit yourself.

When I'm not feeling my best I ask myself, "What are you gonna do about it?" I use the negativity to fuel the transformation into a better me.

Beyoncé

NEGATIVITY CLEAR-OUT

Ask yourself, what are the top three sources of negativity in my life?

Taking each item in turn, what can you do to reduce time with it?

Write small action steps for each item.

Then start with the easiest.

Check back in a week to see how you've got on.

FAKE IT TILL YOU MAKE IT

Imagine yourself as naturally confident and positive. Visualize your relaxed, open posture. See yourself walk into a room with quiet authority, calmly thinking through the task ahead. When the image is clear, step into this person, see the world through their eyes and feel what they feel. The more you do this, the more you'll believe you *are* that person, and soon you won't be pretending any more.

THE ULTIMATE TO-DO LIST

There is nothing more satisfying than writing a list and ticking things off. It makes your day feel manageable, which can help to put your worries to rest and keep you from feeling overwhelmed, and there's a real sense of achievement as you get things done. Here are some tips on making a to-do list work best for you:

- Have a master list – this is where you write every task that occurs to you, whenever it occurs to you. It is the in-tray of lists and stops you worrying you'll forget something. If the task has to be completed by a certain day or time, add that on and underline it.

- Today's top three – from your master list, each morning create a top-three list of things to do today: these can range from must be done to fun quick wins. This is the list you refer back to during the day. Of course, if you finish your list of three, you can always choose more items from the master list, but the key thing is not to overload yourself.

- Be realistic – make sure your Today list is specific and manageable. Not "paint the spare room", but "buy materials for spare room prep" or "choose paint colours".

- Review your Today list – if something moves from list to list and never gets done, take some time to ask yourself why. Is it too big? Can you break it down to smaller tasks and do them over different days?

MAKE TIME
FOR FUN

Schedule time every week to do
something fun. Even if you just
have a window of an hour, write
down something you think you'd
enjoy. Go to see an exhibition, try
a new exercise class or go to the
cinema at 11 a.m.! It's fine to take
along other people, but this is about
what you want to do and can't be
postponed or altered to fit in with
others' plans. It's all about you.

It will never rain roses: when we want to have more roses, we must plant more roses.

George Eliot

Today is a

blank page –

what are you

going to

write on it?

TWENTY MINUTES
OF SUNLIGHT

Did you know that exposure to just 20 minutes
of sunlight a day can promote both vitamin D and
feel-good serotonin production? Of course, take
care to cover up or use sunscreen before your skin
starts to redden. Anyone for lunch in the park?

I CAN DO ANYTHING

if I just
go one step
at a time.

SEA IONS

Sea air is charged with negative ions, which increase the oxygen in our blood and can help to balance our serotonin levels. This is why a trip to the beach or a walk along the coast promotes a good mood and helps you sleep well.

BE A CHILD
AGAIN TODAY AND
SPREAD SOME
MISCHIEF!

RANDOM ACTS OF KINDNESS

A random act of kindness is an unexpected act of helpfulness that will make someone's day better, and they don't only brighten up the recipient's day because you get a boost too! There are opportunities everywhere. Offer to take on a chore for someone. Hold the door for the person behind you or let someone go before you in a queue. Pay for someone's coffee if they have forgotten their purse. And if they ask how they can pay you back, just tell them to pay it forward.

Try to be a rainbow in
someone's cloud.

Maya Angelou

THE POWER OF PETS

Companion animals bring love and laughter into our lives. By giving care and affection you receive even more care and affection back, which brings you comfort and helps to keep worry and loneliness at bay. The routine of care gives a sense of purpose to each day, and can even have health benefits. Walking a dog, for instance, gives you exercise, allows you to get into nature, and they're a great way to connect with other animal lovers. Numerous studies have shown that having a pet has a positive impact on your well-being, so why not visit an animal rescue shelter and see how you might fit a companion animal into your life?

ANIMAL MAGIC

If you can't live with an animal, there are many other ways to connect with them and enjoy the benefits of their companionship:

- Volunteer at an animal rescue centre.

- Appreciate wildlife. Local wildlife trusts run courses on animal identification – from birds to bats, insects to sea life.

- Take a dog for a walk. There are websites and charities where you can "borrow" dogs whose owners need a hand.

Happiness is a
warm puppy.

Charles M. Schulz

LOOKING AFTER THE
POSITIVE MIND

MINDFUL MEDITATION

Mindfulness is something we all do whenever we bring awareness to what we are experiencing. It is about noticing, but not being overwhelmed by, your thoughts and your emotions. Mindful meditation teaches you to do this more often. It has been practised for thousands of years in all parts of the world, but now scientists have proved that it really does make you calmer and happier. Mark Williams, a professor of clinical psychology at Oxford University, says, "Gradually we can train ourselves to notice when our thoughts are taking over, and realise that thoughts are simply "mental events" that do not have to control us." By changing the wiring in our brain, mindfulness can be used to reduce stress and anxiety, treat depression, change body image through self-compassion, improve cognitive function and even help reduce bias such as towards age or race. There are many ways to learn mindful meditation – there are YouTube videos, books and apps which can help, or a great way to learn is to join others – find a class near you and give it a go.

The secret of health for both mind and body is not to mourn for the past, worry about the future, or anticipate troubles, but to live in the present moment wisely and earnestly.

Buddha

TRY T'AI CHI

T'ai chi is a series of slow flowing movements which originated as a martial art in thirteenth-century China. Today in the West it is mostly undertaken as a form of moving meditation, working body, mind and spirit together. T'ai chi can improve muscle strength, flexibility and balance, and you will leave practice both relaxed and energized. There are bound to be classes near you, so why not try it out?

AFFIRMATIONS

Affirmations are simple statements that are designed to incite change or to strengthen us. Whether they serve as inspiration or as simple reminders, they work by reprogramming the subconscious mind to believe a statement.

You can probably still remember negative comments you were given as a child. We learn to believe things that are frequently said to us, so it's easy to think that these negative statements are true – but it's probably not the case! Affirmations use exactly the same mental process, but for the positive. They encourage us to believe good things about ourselves or the world and our place in it. They work best when they are in the first person and positive, with no half measures. Why not give one of these a go:

- I believe in myself.

- I can do anything I set my mind to.

- I choose happiness.

- I can overcome my fears and follow my dreams.

Speak your affirmations aloud every day. It can be first thing in the morning or last thing at night, or you could write one on a Post-it note and leave it by a mirror.

89

LOVE IS ALL AROUND.

MANTRAS

Mantras originally came from Hinduism and Tibetan Buddhism. They are a word or series of words which are repeated to help focus the mind during meditation, and they are often used in yoga. The meaning of the words can influence our subconscious mind and promote positive thoughts – not unlike affirmations!

"Om" is the most sacred mantra in Hinduism and Tibetan Buddhism. It has always been thought to be the sound of the universe – the original vibration – representing birth, death and rebirth. In fact, scientists have proved that it really is the sound of the universe. "Om" vibrates at 432 hertz, which is the universe's natural musical pitch.

Today, however, mantras can be any phrase which will help you with life. Throughout this book you'll find a range of affirmations and positive quotes – choose the one or two that resonate, and repeat them every day. Positivity will follow.

GO CONFIDENTLY IN THE DIRECTION OF YOUR DREAMS. LIVE THE LIFE YOU HAVE IMAGINED.

Henry David Thoreau

I have lived with
several zen masters
— all of them cats.

Eckhart Tolle

CARING TOUCH

Even something as simple as a hug can have a whole host of benefits for your health and well-being. When we hug someone, our body releases oxytocin and our blood pressure drops. A hug also shows someone we care for them, and can strengthen our emotional connection with others. But don't just stop at human touch – stroking or cuddling a pet can have huge benefits for both parties too.

MASSAGE

Having a massage is a great way
to receive caring touch. As well
as releasing muscle tension and
increasing joint mobility, a massage
can affect the chemical balance
in the body by reducing stress
hormones and releasing serotonin
and endorphins, which leaves
you feeling happy and relaxed.

LAUGHTER IS THE BEST MEDICINE

Everyone who has ever laughed (so that's all of us, then) knows how beneficial it is to our mood. Laughter indirectly stimulates endorphins, and after we laugh our blood pressure and heart rate drop, so we feel very relaxed. According to researchers at the University of Michigan, laughing for just 20 seconds could be as good for your lungs as three minutes on a rowing machine. By joking about a shared experience or problem, laughter can increase our sense of belonging. So for a short-term boost and your long-term happiness, find ways to allow yourself to laugh more! Go to see a funny film – they're called "feel good" for a reason. Chat and play with friends' children for a perfect introduction to the joy of silliness. Or, when things get tough and aren't going your way, try laughing at the ridiculous – you might just find it helps.

LAUGHTER CLUBS

While not as prevalent as many types of exercise classes, laughter clubs are a thing. Laughter yoga fuses simulated laughter with deep breathing techniques, encouraging an authentic long and lasting laugh to develop. Other classes use a variety of exercises to create laughter, smiles and letting go. They are great fun, and all have the aim of promoting the release of endorphins. There is even laughter therapy, which assists you in letting go of pent-up unhelpful emotions such as anger and grief. Why not see if you have a class locally that might suit you and give it a go?

ALWAYS LAUGH WHEN YOU CAN; IT IS CHEAP MEDICINE.

Lord Byron

LET THOSE GOOD VIBES ROLL.

READ A BRILLIANT BOOK

The positive power of reading is not to be underestimated! Being able to escape the everyday between the pages of a book has all kinds of benefits for the mind, including reducing symptoms of depression and being as calming as meditation. So, to take a break from the world and refresh your mind: be inspired by a self-help book; dive into non-fiction and have your mind blown by technical innovations, explore the past or marvel at predictions of the future; or find a novel that takes you on an adventure. Every book is a whole world of experience between two covers just waiting to be discovered.

AROMATHERAPY

Essential oils are made from plants and have
been used for thousands of years to stimulate
the brain through your sense of smell. To
give yourself a relaxing aromatherapy session,
put a drop or two of your chosen oil in the
bath, in a diffuser or, for use on the skin, add
a drop to an unperfumed cream or carrier
oil, such as an almond or avocado variety.
Lavender is often used to promote a deep
sleep. Peppermint oil has been associated
with memory and concentration. Clary
sage has long been thought to be uplifting,
and frankincense and rosemary are often
used to relieve stress. An important part of
staying positive is making sure to take care
of yourself. A session of aromatherapy every
once in a while is a great way to press pause
and refresh yourself.

*NB You should not use aromatherapy with
certain medical conditions. Consult your GP
if you are unsure.*

All that I seek is already within me.

Louise Hay

MEDITATE BY THE SEA

Listening to the sound of waves on the beach alters the wave patterns in your brain, which can create a state of deep relaxation. For a natural time-out, head to the sea and feel the benefits of the ocean's rhythm.

I'm

healthier

and

happier

every day.

SELF-COMPASSION

When faced with a setback, or when we don't meet our own expectations, it's easy to be hard on ourselves. Next time a situation like this occurs – if you miss an exercise class or arrive late to work – don't beat yourself up but practise self-compassion. Remind yourself that nobody is perfect, and at least you know how you'd prefer to do things next time. Treat yourself with kindness, and keep going.

I AM
CAPABLE AND
CONFIDENT,
COURAGEOUS
AND BRAVE.

Remember
your strengths

When you are feeling low, remind yourself
of your strengths and what you have
achieved. Think of the challenges you
have faced so far that you have
overcome – if you could beat those,
you can beat whatever else
life throws at you.

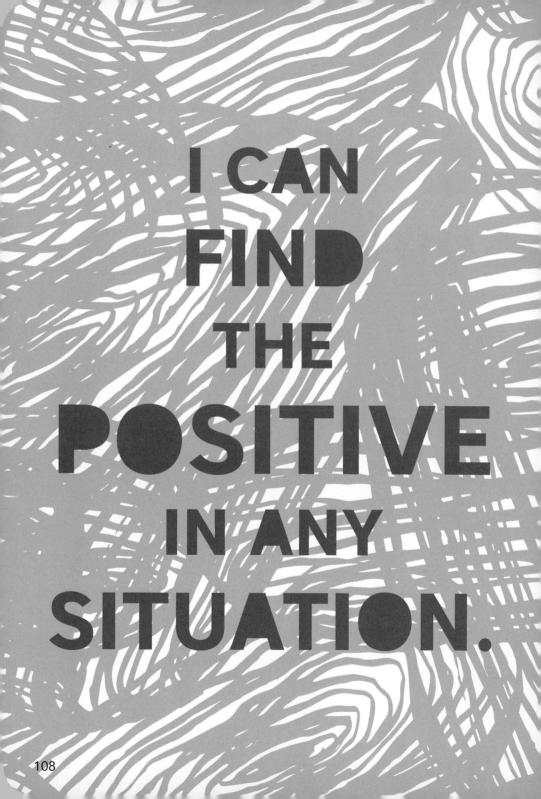

I CAN FIND THE POSITIVE IN ANY SITUATION.

A GOOD NIGHT'S SLEEP

Nothing puts a spring in your step like waking up refreshed, but we don't always prioritize sleep, or when we do it doesn't always come easily. These things can help you achieve your seven to nine optimal hours:

- Set a regular bedtime and waking time. Yes, even at weekends!

- In the day, get outdoors into the fresh air and natural light.

- Limit stimulants such as alcohol and caffeine.

- Exercise regularly (more on this in chapter 7), but not just before going to bed.

- Create a relaxing pre-bedtime routine starting about an hour before you want to go to sleep. Turn off the TV and phone and take a relaxing bath with lavender oil, write in your gratitude journal (see p.15) or read a chapter of a book.

- Increase your levels of sleep-inducing melatonin by keeping your bedroom cool, dark and quiet.

A good laugh and a long sleep are the
best cures in the doctor's book.

Irish proverb

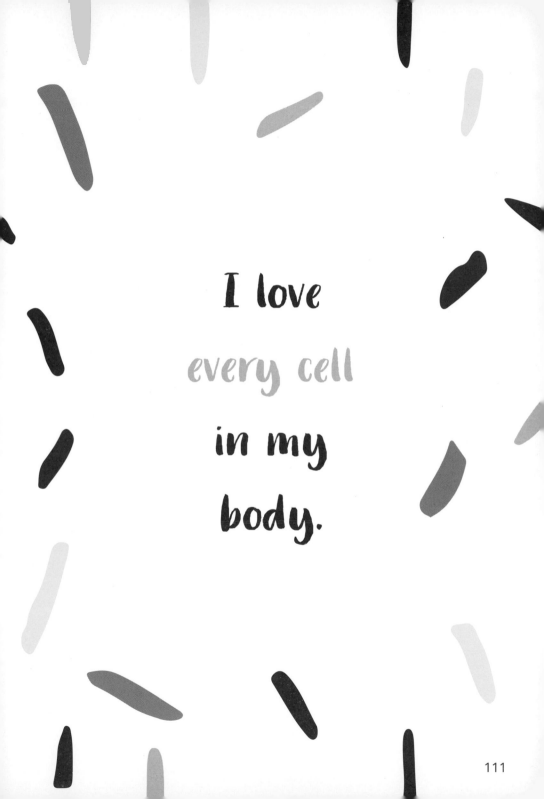

I love

every cell

in my

body.

POSITIVE AND SOCIAL

STAY CONNECTED TO STAY POSITIVE

In 1938 the Harvard Study of Adult Development began. The study involved following the lives of 238 boys from the age of 19 throughout their lives. Some of those same boys are now in their nineties, and they are still part of the study. What the study has found, according to director Robert Waldinger, is that: "people who are more socially connected to family, to friends, to community, are happier, they're physically healthier, and they live longer than people who are less well connected." He explains that if you are more isolated than you want to be, your health and happiness declines. More than employment, money or fame, it is close relationships with friends and family (even if you bicker with them from time to time) that make you happy in the long term. The good news is that it's never too late to reconnect to old friends or to make new ones, and to reap the positive benefits of good relationships.

Of all the things which wisdom provides to make us entirely happy, much the greatest is the possession of friendship.

Epicurus

SEND OUT POSITIVITY

Be positive to other people. Tell friends that you're pleased to see them. Let other people know when they've done well. Sending a card or letter to a friend or family member tells them you took the time to think about them, and they can keep your positive words to return to when they need them. Not only does this help to spread joy in the world, but it will make you feel good too.

NURTURING RELATIONSHIPS

A good relationship with your significant other goes a long way towards giving you a positive outlook on life. Brian Ogolsky researched nearly 60 years' worth of studies about relationships, and found these key strategies for great long-term relationships. Both partners should:

- Think in terms of a team and think about what is best for both of them.

- Be generous, and look for opportunities to carry out random acts of kindness for each other.

- Show gratitude, and make sure the other sees it.

- Pray for, or think compassionately about, their partner.

- Talk about and share chores.

- Discuss their relationship, thinking about where it is going and what can be improved.

- Actually engage with each other – listening and responding.

- Use humour in times of stress.

- Do fun things together.

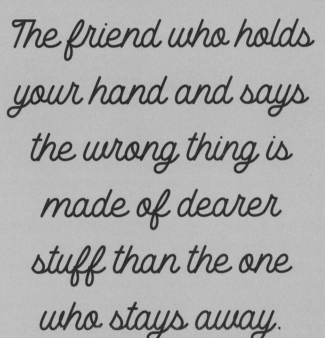

The friend who holds your hand and says the wrong thing is made of dearer stuff than the one who stays away.

Barbara Kingsolver

THANK YOU FOR BEING A FRIEND

While both family and friendship are associated with better health and happiness, a study involving over 270,000 people found that it is friendship that is most beneficial as we advance in age. Another study has found that it is supportive friendships that make the difference. Think about the people you spend time with. Do they lift you up and make you feel good or do you feel drained after spending time with them? Don't be afraid to limit your time with people who bring you down – your well-being and your happiness should be your priority.

The best way to cheer yourself up is to try to cheer somebody else up.

Mark Twain

ADD A LITTLE SPICE

Breaking routine and trying new things can be a great way to give yourself a boost. It could be something small, like trying a new recipe for dinner or going for a walk in the evening rather than sitting in front of the TV. If you're feeling adventurous, you could try new social experiences that have daunted you in the past – volunteer in your community, join a dance group or learn to paint. Doing something a little different to spice up your routine can help to give you a fresher and more positive outlook on life.

SHARE THE FUN WHEREVER YOU GO.

Open up

Our friendships are what buoy us up and keep us going when we're not feeling our best, so don't be afraid to open up and talk about it when you're feeling worried, sad or frustrated. Sharing your feelings with a friend will build trust between you both, and it will make you feel better to share your burden. You may also find your friend has similar stories to share, which will only deepen your bond.

LISTENING TO OTHERS

It's one thing to open up to others when you're feeling down, but listening to friends when they're in the same position is another thing entirely. It can be distressing to listen to others' problems or difficult to stop yourself from taking on their negativity. Here are some tips on how to be a good friend without being overwhelmed, and how to remain positive:

- Try not to judge. If you are thinking negative thoughts about your friend it will come out in your body language. Instead, try to present a positive mindset and expect the best of them.

- Try to understand where they're coming from, but don't support their bad behaviour or they'll have no reason to change. Tell them you prefer to think positively. Avoid being a sympathetic audience for negativity.

- Remember you can't fix their whole life for them. But perhaps there is one thing you can help them think differently about right now.

- Look after yourself. If you're feeling overwhelmed, gently bring the conversation to a close and excuse yourself.

I would rather walk with a friend in the dark, than alone in the light.

Helen Keller

JUST SAY NO

It may sound counterintuitive, but "no" can be a positive word! By saying no to the things you don't want to do or don't have time for, you make time for the things that you care about.

If someone is making unreasonable or unrealistic demands, you don't need to accept them. Nor do you have to say "yes" to every invitation you get, or agree to favours just because you feel you should. Saying yes when you don't mean it will only set you up for failure, increase your stress levels and put strain on your relationships with others. So don't be afraid to say no. You and your time are valuable – be assertive and make your voice heard, and enjoy all the happy benefits!

TRY NEW THINGS

Instead of going to the pub
for the evening, why not try
doing something different with
friends? Play a game – indoors
or outdoors – sign up for a class
or go to a local event. If your
friends aren't keen, or nobody
is free on the evening that you
are, websites such as Meetup or
Citysocializer are there to help
you find like-minded sociable
groups, so you can always try
something new in good company.

LIFE IS ABOUT TAKING PART.

Find a group
of people who
challenge and
inspire you;
spend a lot
of time with
them, and it will
change your life.

Amy Poehler

Don't wait for people to be friendly. Show them how.

SPREAD A SMILE

Sharing a smile is a sure-fire way to
help you feel good. Greet the people
you see, and don't be afraid to smile
at people who pass by, whether
you know them or not. Seeing a
friendly face could make their day,
and it will make you feel great too.

Sometimes
all you need
to do is
be there
and listen.

BE KIND TO COLLEAGUES

You may not know all your colleagues well but a positive working environment makes a difference to everyone. Perhaps she's your boss, or he works on different projects to you – no matter who they are, if you see a colleague having a bad day, think of a small way to help their day improve. Perhaps you could surprise them with a cup of tea or coffee, or offer to take on a job for them. Find a way to make that never-ending bad day just a bit better.

He who sows courtesy reaps friendship, and he who plants kindness gathers love.

Saint Basil of Caesarea

TALK TO SOMEONE NEW.

You could make their day — and they might make yours.

There are no
strangers here;
only friends you
haven't yet met.

W. B. Yeats

EXERCISE FOR POSITIVITY

EXERCISE TO FEEL GOOD

We all know physical activity reduces the risk of many medical conditions – in fact, it can reduce the causes of mortality by up to 30 per cent. But as well as allowing us to live longer lives, it's important to remember just how beneficial exercise is for our mood as well. There are so many ways it has a positive impact on us: physical activity can reduce stress and anxiety and increase confidence and self-esteem; it can boost energy; it increases the production of endorphins, which create positive feelings and ease pain; and it enhances brain sensitivity to the hormones serotonin and norepinephrine, which relieve feelings of depression. Not only does it affect us chemically, but by throwing us "into the moment" it gives us a distraction from our worries, and it can often help us to get a better night's sleep.

Moderate exercise is indispensable; exercise till the mind feels delight in reposing from the fatigue.

Socrates

FIND THE SPORT YOU LOVE

Every type of physical activity benefits us, but for best effects you have to love it. If you don't enjoy running, try tennis. If you don't like tennis, try Zumba. Then try another activity, and another, till you find the one that brings you joy.

THE POSITIVITY PLANK

The plank is a simple, static exercise that strengthens your whole body, but it's particularly good for your core. As you do the exercise you will be able to feel your abdominal muscles tighten, your back strengthening and your posture improving – and, with it, your confidence. Try and maintain this feeling of strength and assurance all day!

You don't need any equipment, and it's simple to do. As long as you have floor space, you can do a plank anywhere, anytime:

- Lie on the floor, and put your hands directly under your shoulders as if you're about to do a press-up. (If you have vulnerable wrists, use your forearms instead.)

- Balance on your toes, and squeeze your glutes to lift and stabilize the body. Your legs, back and neck should now be all in one straight line. Then hold the position.

- Start by holding the plank position for 15 seconds every morning, or just five if that's all you can manage, and then build up by a couple of seconds every day.

EXERCISE MINDFULLY

Bring mindfulness to exercise and observe the results. Listen to the rhythm of your breath as you go and, if you are outside, notice the feeling of the sun or wind on your skin. How does your body feel – what is it finding difficult, what makes it feel good? How has focusing on your body helped? Tuning in to your body will enrich your exercise sessions and help you to understand what you need to do to make you feel your best.

TODAY I WILL

LOVE

MYSELF ENOUGH

TO EXERCISE.

Nothing lifts me out of a bad mood better than a hard workout on my treadmill. It never fails. Exercise is nothing short of a miracle.

Cher

DANCE YOUR WAY TO POSITIVITY

Dance combines physical activity, the creative spirit, emotional expression and social interaction – and what's more, it's fun! And whether it's street dance lessons, ballroom dancing or dancing alone at home in the kitchen, there is a style of dance out there to suit everyone.

GAIN NOT PAIN

You might think that it's best to push yourself to your limits when you're exercising to see the best results, but moderate levels of activity have been shown to suit most people best. Moderate is the level where you can chat while exercising, and your body feels warmer but not very sweaty. You don't have to suffer to boost your body and mind!

JUST A LITTLE BIT

You don't have to commit to hours of exercise every day to feel good. If life is just too hectic, or the thought of a new regime too overwhelming, small amounts of physical activity can still reap huge rewards. Start with just five or ten minutes a few times a week. Take a longer walk on your way to work. Do some gentle exercises at the end of the day. You'll find plenty of apps and YouTube tutorials offering short five-minute workouts for all abilities, so there's something for everyone, whatever stage you're at.

If you get tired, learn to rest,
not to quit.

Banksy

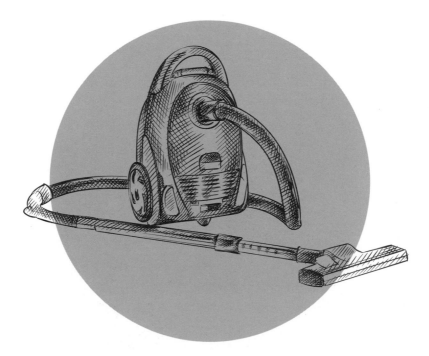

NOT ALL EXERCISE IS "EXERCISE"

It might not be exercise in the traditional sense, but gardening, walking round the shops, DIY and even cleaning can give you a good workout. If you don't have time for more formal exercise, remember that these "chores" offer all the benefits of exercise while you're getting your to-do list done. It's win-win!

Don't count the days: make the days count.

Muhammad Ali

Nobody has ever given their best and regretted it.

PICK YOUR TIME

Take time to find your best time to exercise, and fit it in around your schedule. Things to consider will be when you feel most energised (are you a morning or an evening person?), and what you want your exercise to do. For example, do you want it to be a stress-buster at the end of the day, or something energizing to wake you up?

PARKRUN

Parkrun is a fantastic community event that takes part each week around the world. Each run is five kilometres and is timed, so you can monitor your progress if you wish, although many people take part to enjoy the social aspect and to run with like-minded people. As the name suggests, each event takes place in pleasant parkland. All abilities are encouraged to take part, there is always support from volunteers and it's free! Visit parkrun.org.uk for more information.

I could feel my anger
dissipating as the miles
went by – you can't
run and stay mad!

Kathrine Switzer, Marathon Woman,
first woman to run the Boston
Marathon as a numbered entry

YOU ARE ONLY
ONE WORKOUT
AWAY FROM A
GOOD MOOD.

MAKE IT A GAME

Whatever your chosen physical activity, remember to enjoy it. See how much further you can go this week. Challenge yourself to try a new technique, or to concentrate on just one aspect of the exercise in today's workout. Feel the glow of satisfaction as you learn a new skill and congratulate yourself for a personal best.

Dwell on the
beauty of life.
Watch the
stars, and see
yourself running
with them.

Marcus Aurelius

Just believe in yourself. Even if you don't, pretend that you do and, at some point, you will.

Venus Williams

CONCLUSION

The tips and inspiration in this book are for you to use as you like – feel free to dip in and out, and to try different things on different days. In particular, try to always remember to:

- Practise gratitude.

- Be a good friend.

- Look after yourself both physically and emotionally.

- Look for the beauty in life.

However, if you have found it difficult to stay positive for a long period of time, talk to your doctor about talking therapies or other treatment – asking for help is always, of course, a very positive step.